Better Believe It

Rose Patton

Rose Patton

Better Believe It
30-Day Devotional

By Rose Patton

Rose Patton

Also, by Rose Patton:
The Blessed Bonds Podcast
https://www.buzzsprout.com/2373324

Better Believe It
30-Day Devotional
By Rose Patton

Copyright © 2024 by Rose Patton
All rights reserved.

No part of this book may be reproduced, stored, or transmitted by any means—whether auditory, graphic, mechanical, or electronic—without written permission from the author, except in the case of brief quotations used in articles or reviews.

Published through Amazon Kindle Direct Publishing.

Scripture references are from the **New American Standard Bible**.

Rose Patton

Feel free to connect with me and join the conversation on faith, growth, and community through the podcast and on social media:

- The Blessed Bonds Podcast – https://www.buzzsprout.com/2373324

  Follow me on Instagram – @BLESSED_BONDS1

@BLESSED_BONDS1

Rose Patton

Dedicated to those who are ready to grow in faith and believe in the fullness of God's promises.

Rose Patton

Dear Friends,

This book is a reflection of the journey God has led me on, and I'm honored to share it with you. I want to start by saying—I'm not perfect. This book isn't perfect. It wasn't crafted by a team of editors or polished to some unreachable standard. It's simply the message that has been laid on my heart, written for you in the most honest way I know how.

What this book isn't is a masterpiece of grammar or an example of flawless writing. You might notice typos or a misplaced comma here and there, and that's okay. My focus was never on perfection but on making sure you receive what's inside these pages. This message is far too important to let perfectionism hold it back.

So if you spot an imperfection, I hope it serves as a gentle nudge for you to embrace doing things messy sometimes. Don't let fear of not having it all together stop you from sharing your gifts, your heart, and your story.

Rose Patton

It's not about how it looks on the outside; it's about the difference it can make on the inside.

This book is about stepping into who God has called you to be and letting Him lead—even when it feels messy or imperfect. It's about growth, grace, and transformation. My prayer is that it resonates deeply with you and encourages you to move forward, knowing that the world needs what you have to offer, just as you are.

Let's journey together.

With love and gratitude,

Rose Patton

Rose Patton

Table of Contents

Day 1: Loved Beyond Measure | 19

Day 2: Live Today Like It's Your Last | 24

Day 3: Is Honesty Really That Important? | 29

Day 4: Relationship, Not Religion | 34

Day 5: How to Talk to Others About God | 39

Day 6: Tempted by the Devil | 45

Day 7: Stop Judging People| 51

Day 8: Be a Friend Like Jesus | 56

Day 9: Worshiping God | 61

Day 10: They Might Hate You, But God Chose You | 66

Day 11: Discipline Yourself for Christ | 71

Day 12: Finding God in the Struggle | 76

Day 13: Chasing After Things of This World| 81

Day 14: Does Who I Date Really Matter? | 86

Day 15: Finding Faith Every Day | 91

Day 16: Why It's Important to Be in Your Bible |	96
Day 17: Learning to Be Patient |	101
Day 18: Learning to Respect Others |	106
Day 19: Trusting God |	112
Day 20: The Power of Asking for Help |	117
Day 21: Walk Away |	122
Day 22: Failing Forward |	128
Day 23: Why Prayer Is So Powerful |	133
Day 24: Being Content |	138
Day 25: God's Approval vs. The World's Approval |	143
Day 26: You Are Forgiven |	148
Day 27: Praise the Lord |	153
Day 28: Love Like Jesus |	158
Day 29: God Will Give You Strength |	163
Day 30: There Is Always Hope |	168

Where Are You Right Now?

Before you dive into this devotional, take a moment to pause and reflect. Where are you in your walk with Christ? Use this space to jot down your thoughts, feelings, and where you see yourself in your faith journey right now. These notes will be a beautiful reminder of where you started, so you can look back and see how far you've come by the end of this devotional.

Notes:

_____
_____
_____
_____
_____
_____
_____
_____
_____
_____
_____

Rose Patton

Notes:

Rose Patton

Notes:

Rose Patton

Notes:

Rose Patton

Notes:

Rose Patton

Notes:

Rose Patton

"That's the thing about God; He's the one in charge: not you or me."

— Sadie Robertson

Day 1

Loved Beyond Measure

I have a friend who once texted me and said she didn't feel loved. That broke my heart because I know how much God loves us. So, I reminded her that the Creator of the world loves her. And I want to remind you that Jesus literally died on a cross for you! You don't die for someone unless you love them. If that boy or girl doesn't love you, that's okay—because God loves you. No one will ever love you like God does. His love never fails.

John 3:16 says, *"For God so loved the world, that He gave His only begotten Son, that whoever believes in Him shall not perish, but have eternal life."* God literally loves us all so much that He sent Jesus here to die for us. Think about that: someone died for you because they love you so much and want you to be with them for eternity.

Romans 5:8 reminds us, *"But God demonstrates His own love toward us, in that while we were sinners, Christ died for us."* Even though we are sinners and don't deserve His love, He still loves us. We could never earn or deserve God's love, yet He gives it to us every single day. No matter what you've done or where you go, He will always give you never-ending love and forgiveness.

1 Peter 5:7 says, *"casting all your anxiety on Him, because He cares for you."* God cares about you so much that He tells you to put all your worries and anxieties in His hands. Whatever you're going through, tell Him about it and ask Him for help. He loves and cares about you so much that He promises never to leave you.

1 John 4:8 says, *"The one who does not love does not know God, for God is love."* God isn't just loving or full of love—He is the very definition of love. His nature defines what love is, and everything we understand about true, selfless, and pure love comes from Him. Without God, there is no love, because love

begins and ends with Him. He doesn't simply feel love; He is the source and meaning of love itself.

Sometimes, the world is so hateful that we feel like we aren't loved. But God's love is different from any love in the world. His love never changes. No matter what you do, He still loves you. Remember, you are loved, even if you sometimes don't feel like it.

Challenge: Today, write down three ways you've felt God's love in your life this week.

Dive in Deeper: Jeremiah 31:3, Lamentations 3:22-23, Isaiah 54:10.

Notes:

"Two-thirds of God's name is GO. Stop delaying, overthinking, and waiting for applause. Take action—not for others, but for clarity and growth."

— Eileen Wilder

Day 2

Live Today Like It's Your Last

Have you ever put something off or said, "I'll do it later"? Yeah, I have too. But the thing is, if God puts a purpose or a dream in your heart, then you need to go out and do what God is telling you to do. God placed these dreams in your heart today; if He wanted you to do it tomorrow, why would He have put them in your heart today? The truth is, you don't know if you'll wake up tomorrow.

I want you to know that you can change so many people's lives. You never know when your time here on earth will come to an end. The truth is, if you share God's word with people who are not believers, you might help save them. God is the only one who can save, but you can help. Take charge of every opportunity to share God's word because that might be the conversation that changes their life.

Proverbs 27:1: *"Do not boast about tomorrow, for you do not know what a day may bring forth."*
This verse really makes you sit back and think about how you've been living. To me, this verse is very straightforward. As humans, we tend to be boastful, but here, it tells us not to be. My best advice for you is this: be proud of your life and what you've accomplished, but don't be prideful. You wouldn't have accomplished it without God. Give Him the glory.

Matthew 24:44: *"For this reason, you also must be ready; for the Son of Man is coming at an hour when you do not think He will."*
This reminds us that we don't know exactly when Jesus is coming back. So be ready! Share God's word and help bring others closer to Him. Jesus might come back tomorrow, so you need to be prepared.

James 4:14: *"Yet you do not know what your life will be like tomorrow. You are just a vapor that appears for a little while and then vanishes away."*
This verse is so incredible! It really helps you see your life for what it truly is. Now, I don't

want you to think this verse is saying you aren't important—because let me tell you, you are so important! To me, this verse emphasizes that our lives go by so fast, and we need to soak up every moment. You never know which moment might be your last. Take advantage of every situation and let everything you do be for His glory.

Challenge: Today share God's word with one new person today, even if it feels uncomfortable. Be grateful for today because tomorrow might not come.

Dive in Deeper: Isaiah 55:6, Luke 12:19-20, 2 Corinthians 6:2.

Rose Patton

Notes:

"You tell people how to treat you by what you accept."

— Trent Shelton

Day 3

Is Honesty Really That Important?

Sometimes, you will want to lie. Because lying feels like the easy way out. But Jesus didn't do what was easy when He died on the cross— He did what God called Him to do. And God has called us to be truthful, so be that. It may be hard, but trust me, so was dying on the cross. Yet Jesus still did it. So I promise you, you can be truthful and honest.

Proverbs 12:22 says, *"Lying lips are an abomination to the Lord, but those who deal faithfully are His delight."* God hates lying, and part of me thinks that's because He sees the full effect it has on others. You might tell a small lie that you think won't hurt anyone. Maybe it won't hurt you, but you have no idea if it hurt someone else.

Ephesians 4:25 says, *"Therefore, laying aside falsehood, speak truth each one of you with his neighbor, for we are members of one another."* Being truthful is so important. I've seen relationships and friendships crumble because they lacked honesty. We were created to love one another, but when we lie, we destroy trust. And some people find it hard to love someone they can't trust.

Psalm 15:1-2 says, *"O Lord, who may abide in Your tent? Who may dwell on Your holy hill? He who walks with integrity and works righteousness, and speaks truth in his heart."*

When we live truthfully, we reflect God's character. God is the ultimate truth—His word is pure, and His promises are always trustworthy. By being truthful, we mirror that in our own lives. Honesty isn't just a personal choice; it's a way to honor God and show others what His love and integrity look like in action.

A lot of times, we lie to ourselves. We try to make ourselves believe something that isn't true because the truth might hurt. But when we're honest with ourselves, we can start to change for God. When you admit where you're falling short and acknowledge that you need help, you'll be able to accept God's forgiveness—and you will be saved.

Challenge: This week, focus on being completely honest in all your conversations. Before you speak, pause and ask yourself, "Is this truthful?" Even if honesty feels uncomfortable, choose truth over convenience. At the end of each day, reflect on moments when being truthful was challenging but rewarding. Write down what you learned from these experiences and how it strengthened your relationships or your faith.

Dive in Deeper: Leviticus 19:11, Proverbs 11:3, Exodus 20:16.

Rose Patton

Notes:

"I would rather stand with God and be judged by the world than to stand with the world and be judged by God."
— Unknown

Day 4

Relationship, Not Religion

This is something my youth pastor has told me many times: just because you go to church and call yourself a Christian doesn't mean you know Christ. Someone once told me, *"There will be people in Hell who never smoked, never cussed, who went to church every Sunday but never gave their life to Christ."* That changed my whole view on my relationship with Christ. I realized I didn't want to just say that I knew of Christ—I wanted to truly know Him.

Someone once asked me, *"Rose, do you actually know God, or do you just know churchy words?"* And that was a game changer for me. I had been living for people to think I had my relationship with God all figured out. But then I started living to actually have a relationship with God and truly know Him.

Colossians 2:6-7 says, *"Therefore as you have received Christ Jesus the Lord, so walk in Him, having been firmly rooted and now being built up in*

Him and established in your faith, just as you were instructed, and overflowing with gratitude." There will be things in your life that try to distract you from God, and situations where you feel like you're fighting on your own. But once you firmly plant your faith in Christ, you will experience an overwhelming peace. I'm not saying you won't go through hard times—you will. But you have the Creator of everything on your side. Never doubt God's strength.

Philippians 3:8 says, *"More than that, I count all things to be loss in view of the surpassing value of knowing Christ Jesus my Lord, for whom I have suffered the loss of all things and count them but rubbish so that I may gain Christ."* When you face judgment, it's not going to matter how many trophies you've won. What will matter is your relationship with Christ.

John 15:4-5 says, *"Abide in Me, and I in you. As the branch cannot bear fruit of itself unless it abides in the vine, so neither can you unless you abide in Me. I am the vine, you are the branches; he who abides in Me and I in him, bears much fruit, for apart from Me you can do nothing."* I love this verse! Christ reminds us that when we are close to Him, we will flourish, becoming who He created us to be. But we cannot do anything without Him. I can testify to this truth. When I'm not in God's Word or when I've been distant from Christ, I start to doubt the power within me. The enemy will try to convince you that you don't need God, but let me tell you—you NEED God. Your relationship with Christ is the most important relationship you will ever have. Never let anyone or anything distract you from Him.

Challenge: Today, I challenge you to take a moment to evaluate your relationship with Christ. Ask yourself, Do I know God, or just know of Him? Spend time in prayer, asking God to help you grow closer to Him and reconnect if you've been distant.

Dive in Deeper: Revelation 3:20, 2 Corinthians 5:17, and John 14:6.

Rose Patton

Notes:

"Imagine in heaven one day someone walks up to you and says, 'I am here because you weren't ashamed to share Jesus with people, so thank you.'"

— Unknown

Day 5

How to Talk to Others About God

Matthew 28:19-20: *"Go therefore and make disciples of all the nations, baptizing them in the name of the Father and the Son and the Holy Spirit, teaching them to observe all that I commanded you; and lo, I am with you always, even to the end of the age."* I want to point out the fact that this verse starts by saying "Go." It doesn't say "go tomorrow," so don't wait until tomorrow to share God's word. Do that today, because you are never guaranteed tomorrow. Jesus reminds us that He is with us until the end. He doesn't ever want us to feel like we are doing anything alone. Because we aren't alone—we have Him. When you are telling others about God, make sure you ask Him what He wants you to say. You aren't the one speaking; it's God through you.

Mark 16:15: *"And He said to them, 'Go into all the world and preach the gospel to all creation.'"*

Here, Jesus is talking to His disciples. He was giving them a mission, and He has given you the same mission—to share His word.

Romans 1:16: *"For I am not ashamed of the gospel, for it is the power of God for salvation to everyone who believes, to the Jew first and also to the Greek."* I want you to be like this when you are sharing the word. Do not be ashamed. Trust me, people will make fun of you, but so what? It doesn't change the way God loves you. It can be hard to share the word with our friends who aren't believers, but pray about it and just go tell them what you know. It may not be perfect, but it's not supposed to be perfect— it's supposed to be honest. Don't be afraid for people to make fun of you or for your friends to leave you. This is what God is calling you to do.

2 Timothy 4:2: *"Preach the word; be ready in season and out of season; reprove, rebuke, exhort, with great patience and instruction."* This is a really good reminder that we need to always be ready to share God's word and His love. Because you never know when someone is going to need

to hear about God. This also reminds us that we need to have great patience and instruction. Be patient when you are sharing God's word. Be kind and loving.

Matthew 5:14: *"You are the light of the world. A city set on a hill cannot be hidden."* And verse 16: *"Let your light shine before men in such a way that they may see your good works and glorify your Father who is in heaven."* This is such an awesome verse. "You are the light of the world"—that is so true, and you need to remember that. Sometimes, the enemy tries to show you all the darkness in the world, making you feel like your light isn't enough. But let me tell you, God's light is brighter than any darkness! So, do not ever be afraid to shine His light through you.

Challenge: For today's challenge, I want you to talk to one person about God and His love. Set out and find one person a day, and if you do this every day for a year, you will have told 365 people about God. As you go on, you will become more confident in sharing His word.

Dive in Deeper: Psalm 96:2-3, Colossians 4:5-6, 1 Peter 3:15

Rose Patton

Notes:

"Everything you're going through will soon turn into everything you made it through."
— Trent Shelton

Day 6

Tempted by the Devil

I know how it feels to be tempted by the devil. You might feel alone, like you're the only one struggling. Or you might feel like you can't talk to anyone because you're ashamed. And there are different kinds of temptations—maybe you're tempted to steal, lie, or cheat. I get it. But you're going to be alright!

I'm going to share some things that helped me. If you feel like you can't talk to anyone, talk to God. I know it's hard as humans to admit to others when we're messing up. But God isn't just anyone; He is your Creator. He knew you before you knew you. And that's wild, right? Because we all have certain things we hide from people, especially from the ones we love, since we don't want anyone to be disappointed in us.

But God knows all of your flaws. Those things you hide from everyone—those things you don't want anyone to see—God sees them. And He doesn't love you any less.

Here are some things that helped me a lot: If you aren't comfortable talking to anyone else, talk to God! He wants you to repent and admit your sins to Him. Trust me, it will help you feel better.

Don't ignore the temptation, but flee from it. You may feel like you can't escape your sin or temptation, but read 1 Corinthians 10:13: *"No temptation has overtaken you but such as is common to man; and God is faithful, who will not allow you to be tempted beyond what you are able, but with the temptation will provide the way to escape also, so that you will be able to endure it."*

This verse shook me. I felt like I was useless and would never be able to escape my temptation. But when I read this verse, I was brought to my knees in tears. It reassured me that God would help me and that I am never alone.

This verse also reminded me that I'm not fighting this battle alone. I have the Most High God on my side. When Jesus died on the cross, He won every battle you will ever go through. But you have to choose to trust Him.

Luke 15:4 says: *"What man among you, if he has a hundred sheep and has lost one of them, does not leave the ninety-nine in the open pasture and go after the one which is lost until he finds it?"*

And verse 7 says:*"I tell you that in the same way, there will be more joy in heaven over one sinner who repents than over ninety-nine righteous persons who need no repentance."*

These verses show us that Jesus will find us, no matter how far He has to go or how much He has to do, because He loves us. There is nowhere you can go that God isn't. He wants a relationship with you. I mean, He wouldn't have created you if He didn't want you.

So no matter what you do, always come back to Him.

Matthew 4:7 says:*"Jesus said to him, 'On the other hand, it is written, you shall not put the Lord your God to the test.'"*

Don't test how far God will go to save you. You need to come to Him, repent, and allow Him to save you. God is the only one who can save you. That boy or that girl cannot save you—only God. So go to Him.

Challenge: Today, write down your biggest temptation and a prayer asking for God's strength to overcome it.

Dive in Deeper: Romans 8:13, Luke 22:40, James 1:16, James 4:7-8

Rose Patton

Notes:

*"**Life with God is not immunity from difficulties but peace within difficulties.**"*

— *C.S. Lewis*

Day 7

Stop Judging People

First of all, I want to explain what I mean by "judging people" since this could mean different things. Today, we will be talking about how God has called us to love one another instead of judging one another.

Judging someone could look like criticizing their style or clothing. It could also mean judging the situations they're in or what their lives look like to you. Lastly, it could mean judging their personality or trying to make someone change just because they aren't exactly like you.

I want to remind you that you were not called to this world to be like the world but to be like Jesus. Jesus tells us to love one another, not to judge one another. Let God be the judge. You have no clue what anyone else is going through, but God does. Instead of being the person who judges others, be the person who loves them. You might be the only bit of love some people see in their lives.

Instead of spending your time tearing someone down with judgment, spend your time praying for them, inviting them to church, and being there for them.

Romans 14:10 says, *"But you, why do you judge your brother? Or you again, why do you regard your brother with contempt? For we will all stand before the judgment seat of God."* This verse clearly tells us that God will be our judge. We have no right to judge anyone—let God be the judge. He will always be right.

If we look at James 4:12: *"There is only one Lawgiver and Judge, the One who is able to save and destroy; but who are you to judge your neighbor?"* That last part gets me: *"Who are you to judge your neighbor?"* We don't have any business judging anyone. Leave that to God.

Luke 6:31 says, *"Treat others the same way you want them to treat you."* This reminds me that we shouldn't judge others because we wouldn't want to be judged ourselves. Treat everyone with love, because that's how you would want to be treated.

I've learned the hard way that when I judged people, they judged me back. And that hurt because I started to feel the pain I was causing others. So instead, I chose to love them—even when they didn't love me back. By doing that, I can now be a role model and show others how to love instead of judge.

Challenge: Take a moment today to ask yourself: "Where in my life have I been quick to judge?" Pray and ask God to help you replace judgment with love.

Dive in Deeper: James 4:11, Matthew 7:1-6, Luke 6:37

Rose Patton

Notes:

"The best way to make friends is to be friendly."
— Ashlee Latimer

Day 8

Be a Friend Like Jesus

Your friends are so important! I absolutely love all my friends and am so grateful to have them. They help me grow closer to God and push me to keep trying. Being there for them and helping them grow their relationship with Christ is so important. We aren't meant to go through life by ourselves.

James 5:16 says, *"Therefore, confess your sins to one another, and pray for one another so that you may be healed. The effective prayers of a righteous man can accomplish much."* Something I do a lot for my friends is pray for them or with them. No matter how perfect their lives may seem, I know they have hurt in their lives, and I want to be there for them so they can get through that.

Galatians 6:2 says, *"Bear one another's burdens, and thereby fulfill the law of Christ."* Life gets really hard when you try to bear everything on your own. You have to give it all to God, and the cool thing is that God will give us people who will help us so we don't have to carry all our burdens by ourselves. Your friends can't bear it all on their own. They need you. So be there for them. Help them grow closer to God, and hold tight to them when they are struggling.

Proverbs 17:17 says, *"A friend loves at all times, and a brother is born for adversity."* Sometimes, it's hard to love others. But think about the fact that God still loves you, even when you mess up. You might be the only bit of love some people have in their lives. Take advantage of that and use it to share God's love.

1 Thessalonians 5:11 says, *"Therefore encourage one another and build up one another, just as you also are doing."* We all need a little help and encouragement sometimes. You never know what someone else is going through. There are already enough people in the world who will tear them down. Instead of joining them, encourage and build others up. You never know how much someone needs the love you

have to share. Be the kind of friend that Jesus is to you.

Challenge: Today, I challenge you to text a friend and check on them. See if they need anything or if they need any prayer.

Dive in Deeper: Hebrews 3:13, Hebrews 10:24–25, Ecclesiastes 4:9–10.

Rose Patton

Notes:

"God didn't give them the vision, so stop expecting them to see it."
— Trent Shelton

Day 9

Worshiping God

Whenever people ask me why I praise God, I tell them, "Because He is worthy of all of my praise." In fact, He is worthy of way more than I can give Him. God has been there for me no matter how far I ran, and He has changed and saved my life. I know I wouldn't have made it this far without God, so I choose to worship and praise Him.

Psalm 145:3: *"Great is the Lord, and highly to be praised; His greatness is unsearchable."* The Lord is truly so good! He is so loving and forgiving, no matter what we do. We will never be able to deserve God's love or forgiveness, yet He gives it to us unconditionally. That is true love.

Psalm 19:1: *"The heavens are telling of the glory of God; and the expanse is declaring the work of His hands."* If we just take a second to look around, we can see how wonderful God is. Whenever I look at the sunrise, I am reminded of how wonderful God is. He creates so many beautiful things, like you.

Revelation 4:11: *"Worthy are You, our Lord and our God, to receive glory and honor and power; for You created all things, and because of Your will, they existed and were created."* Have you ever thanked God for creating you? One time I thought about this. The crazy thing is that God created us uniquely and beautifully. Yet, we still complain about how He created us, and we get mad when we go through difficult situations. But God created you for a purpose, and He deserves your praise.

Psalm 34:1-2: *"I will bless the Lord at all times; His praise shall continually be in my mouth. My soul will make its boast in the Lord; the humble will hear it and rejoice."* We should boast of God, not of ourselves. Don't tell people about you—tell people about God. A lot of times, we boast about how good we are, but instead, we should learn to boast about how good God has been in our lives.

Praise God because He has been so good. And we know that He will always be good, no matter the circumstances.

Challenge: Today, I want you to make a worship playlist and add some of your favorite worship songs so that you can worship and praise God.

Dive in Deeper: 1 Chronicles 16:34, Isaiah 55:12, Psalm 103:1.

Rose Patton

Notes:

"Stop caring about what other people think of you. Jesus was literally perfect and people still hated Him."
— *Unknown*

Day 10

They Might Hate You, But God Chose You

I feel like sometimes we think a little too much about what others think of us. I totally understand the feeling of wanting to be liked by others. But the only opinion that really matters is God's. And that has taken me a while to realize. Instead of thinking about what others say about you, think about what God says about you. Ephesians 1:4 tells us that we are chosen! God chose you because you are unique and beautiful in your own way. God has called you here for a reason, no matter what the world says.

Matthew 10:22 says, *"You will be hated by all because of My name, but it is the one who has endured to the end who will be saved."* This verse reminds me that we will be hated and disliked for being followers of Christ, but we should not hate other people. Instead, we should move forward every day and share the love of

Christ. It also reminds me not to get caught up in caring about being hated but to live the life God has called you to live. People are going to judge you anyway.

John 15:18-19 says, *"If the world hates you, you know that it has hated Me before it hated you. If you were of the world, the world would love its own; but because you are not of the world, but I chose you out of the world, because of this the world hates you."* Christ reminds us that we are His. We aren't called to be like this world. This world is mean and unloving and hateful. But we are called to be like Christ—He is loving, forgiving, and altogether wonderful. I am so glad that we are called to be like Christ instead of the world.

1 John 3:13 says, *"Do not be surprised, brethren, if the world hates you."* This makes me think about the fact that it doesn't really matter if others like you or not. Because I'm here to tell you that there are going to be people who hate you. But guess what? That doesn't change the fact that Jesus still died on the cross for you. Haters are going to come and go, and what I say is: "You can't control what people say to

you, but you can control how you take it."
The enemy tells you lies; God tells you truth. It's your choice who you listen to. Choose wisely.

It's not your job to make people like you. Be loving to all people, but know that not all people will love you back. Don't let other people's opinions of you change your opinion of yourself.

Challenge: Today, I challenge you to write down five things you love about yourself and why you love them.

Dive in Deeper: 2 Timothy 3:12, John 16:33, Matthew 5:10-12.

Rose Patton

Notes:

"Your talent is God's gift to you. What you do with it is your gift back to God."

— Leo Buscaglia

Day 11

Discipline Yourself for Christ

Discipline is something that can make or break your future. Someone once told me, "You're as close to Christ as you choose to be." If you want to strengthen your relationship with Christ, that's on you. Nobody else can do that for you.

Proverbs 25:28 says, *"Like a trampled spring and a polluted well is a righteous man who gives way before the wicked."* If you don't discipline yourself for God, then you will be easily tricked and distracted. If you aren't in the Bible and in prayer, how will you know what is true and what is a lie? You won't.

Hebrews 12:11 says, *"All discipline for the moment seems not to be joyful, but sorrowful; yet to those who have been trained by it, afterwards it yields the peaceful fruit of righteousness."* A lot of times, being disciplined isn't easy. But that shows how much you truly care about what you are being disciplined in. I've learned that we make time for what we care about. So take time to grow your relationship with Christ.

Deuteronomy 8:5 says, *"Thus you are to know in your heart that the Lord your God was disciplining you just as a man disciplines his son."* God will discipline us so we can do the work He has called us to do. Discipline is sometimes hard to go through, but it helps form you into the person God needs you to be. Allow God to discipline you for His good.

Proverbs 13:18 says, *"Poverty and shame will come to him who neglects discipline, but he who regards reproof will be honored."* When we neglect discipline or choose not to discipline ourselves, we won't prosper or grow. But when you choose to discipline yourself, you choose to grow and change your life.

2 Timothy 1:7 says, *"For God has not given us a spirit of timidity, but of power and love and discipline."* God gave us this spirit, but it's our choice whether we tap into it or not. You can choose to listen to God, discipline yourself for Him, and grow your relationship with Him, or you can choose to ignore Him and

push Him away. If you do, you'll end up wasting your life chasing things that pull you further from Him.

We should discipline ourselves to be in the Bible and to spend time with God. Too often, we choose to watch a movie, play video games, or scroll on our phones instead of spending time with Him. Please don't waste your life on things that won't grow you closer to God.

Challenge:
Today, I challenge you to turn off all social media notifications and avoid opening any social media. Instead of watching a movie or playing video games, spend that time growing your relationship with God—whether that's singing worship music, reading your Bible, or praying. Find a way to spend time with God without distractions. It will be so worth it—trust me.

Dive in Deeper: Proverbs 1:7, Proverbs 12:1, Revelation 3:19.

Rose Patton

Notes:

"You have survived 100% of your bad days."
— Unknown

Day 12

Finding God in the Struggle

While I was injured, I became mad at God. I kept asking Him, "Why me?" or "Why is this happening?" I was so mad that I couldn't swim. It was so hard for me, and so I blamed it on God. But now I look back and thank God for making me take a break from swimming so I could realize that He is more important than swimming.

Psalm 23:4: *"Even though I walk through the valley of the shadow of death, I fear no evil, for You are with me; Your rod and Your staff, they comfort me."* This reminds me that God is there for us through every struggle and every valley we go through. No matter how hard things get, God will never leave you.

Romans 8:28: *"And we know that God causes all things to work together for good to those who love God, to those who are called according to His purpose."* I love this verse. It's a great reminder that even if we don't understand what God is doing in our lives right now, He is doing it for good. While I was injured, I didn't understand why that was happening, but now I am grateful I went through it because my relationship with God is so much stronger. He just had to remove a distraction from my life.

Jeremiah 29:11: *"For I know the plans I have for you," declares the Lord, "plans for welfare and not for calamity, to give you a future and a hope."* This is an excellent reminder that God knows what He is doing. Trust Him—His plan is way better.

1 Thessalonians 5:16-18: *"Rejoice always; pray without ceasing; in everything give thanks; for this is God's will for you in Christ Jesus."* No matter how hard it is right now, rejoice! Life might not be perfect at this moment, but God is perfect at every moment. And you have Him on your side. He has already won the battle. You're never fighting alone!

James 1:2-3: *"Consider it all joy, my brethren, when you encounter various trials, knowing that the testing of your faith produces endurance."* Ahhhh, I love this verse so much. And you will probably see me bring it up often. This can help remind us that, yes, we will have trials, but we will grow from those trials. Remember, tests become testimonies! Keep pushing through and trusting God the whole way; have faith in His plan.

Challenge: Today, take a moment to reflect on a difficult situation in your life. Write down how God might have used that challenge to strengthen your faith or bring you closer to Him. Thank Him for being with you through it all.

Dive in Deeper: Romans 5:3-5, 2 Corinthians 12:9-10, Philippians 4:4-7

Rose Patton

Notes:

"Chasing the things of this world will never fulfill you, but chasing after God will."
— *Unknown*

Day 13

Chasing After Things of This World

Sometimes, we get so focused on what the world can give us. We get distracted by all the material things around us and lose sight of what truly matters: God. I've seen so many people get wrapped up in chasing money and the idea of being rich, thinking that wealth will solve all their problems, forgetting what is truly valuable—the peace, joy, and purpose that only God can provide.

Proverbs 23:4-5 says, *"Do not weary yourself to gain wealth, cease from your consideration of it. When you set your eyes on it, it is gone. For wealth certainly makes itself wings like an eagle that flies toward the heavens."* Wealth comes and goes, so don't spend your life chasing after it. One day, it will all vanish and no longer matter.

Hebrews 13:5 reminds us, *"Make sure that your character is free from the love of money, being content with what you have; for He Himself has said, 'I will never desert you, nor will I ever forsake you.'"* This verse reminds me that no amount of money can make us feel loved, bring us peace, or be there when we need it. Only God can do all those things. It's easy to get caught up in what we don't have, but when we stop and reflect, we see that the blessings we do have—health, relationships, and, most importantly, God's presence—are more than enough. Be content with what you've been given, knowing that God is always with you.

Colossians 3:2 says, *"Set your mind on the things above, not on the things that are on earth."* This verse sums it up perfectly. It's one we should always remember. We need to set our minds on God and nurture our relationship with Him instead of focusing on worldly things that ultimately won't matter.

Live your life for God, not earthly things. In the end, it won't matter how much money you made or how many trophies you won—they will no longer have any value. You can't pay your way into heaven. Live for God, not the world.

Challenge: Today's challenge is to write down ten things you are grateful for. Reflect on the ways God has blessed you, and discover how much better He is than anything this world can offer.

Dive in Deeper: Matthew 6:33, James 4:4, 1 John 2:15-17

Rose Patton

Notes:

"Don't let a man who doesn't even read his Bible separate you from the man who wrote the Bible."

— Unknown

Day 14

Does Who I Date Really Matter?

This is a question that a lot of my friends have asked me. I believe that it really does matter. The Bible doesn't specifically talk about dating—it talks about marriage. We should date with the intention of marrying, not just to date for fun or companionship.

As I've gotten older, many of my friends tell me, "I'm looking for someone to date." But if you're simply looking for a boyfriend or girlfriend, that's exactly what you'll find—and that's all they'll ever be. You don't need to search for someone to date; God has already chosen the one for you.

Matthew 6:33 says, *"But seek first His kingdom and His righteousness, and all these things will be added to you."* This verse is such a good reminder that when we seek God and follow Him, everything else will fall into place. Once you have a strong relationship with God, you'll be able to build a strong relationship with someone else.

2 Corinthians 6:14 tells us, *"Do not be bound together with unbelievers; for what partnership have righteousness and lawlessness, or what fellowship has light with darkness?"* This is a verse that one of my close friends often shares with me. It reminds us that as believers, we should be bound together with other believers.

Sometimes people say, "But maybe I can change him." Yes, you can have an impact on someone else's life and help bring them closer to Christ. But you must also remember that they can pull you away from Christ just as easily.

Proverbs 4:23 says, *"Watch over your heart with all diligence, for from it flow the springs of life."* Your heart is a masterpiece—start treating it like it is. Protect it as if it's one of a kind, because it is. If someone is hurting you or pulling you away from God, don't be afraid to walk away. You won't be lonely; you have God.

One thing I often tell people is to make sure your heart is full before entering a relationship. If your heart is full of God's love, then you'll have love to give. If your heart is broken and empty, you're more likely to settle for less than you deserve. You won't have love to give, either. Work on your relationship with God before stepping into any other relationships.

Challenge: Make a list of qualities you would like in a future spouse. Then, compare that list to your current priorities. Are you seeking God and His kingdom first, or are you prioritizing something else?

Dive in Deeper: 1 Thessalonians 4:3-5, Ephesians 5:21, 1 Corinthians 13:4-7

Rose Patton

Notes:

Not every day is good, but there is something good in every day."
— Alice Morse Earle

Day 15

Finding Faith Every Day

I know it can be hard to have faith sometimes. As humans, we tend to doubt other people. But you have no reason to doubt God. I can testify that He never leaves you. He will hold you through your darkest valleys and never let you go. There will be times in your life here on earth when you start to wonder if God is there for you. But that's the enemy trying to distract you from God. Even in the rough patches, learn to praise Him and have faith that, even though you don't know the answer, He does.

James 1:2-3 says, *"Consider it all joy, my brethren, when you encounter various trials, knowing that the testing of your faith produces endurance."* I want you to remember this verse when you're going through hard times. Everything you are facing is making you stronger, and you will have a story to share once you've made it through.

What you're going through today will one day be the testimony of what you've overcome.

Hebrews 11:1 tells us, *"Now faith is the assurance of things hoped for, the conviction of things not seen."* I once did a podcast with someone, and we talked about how we have faith in God. We might not see God physically on earth right now, but that doesn't mean He isn't here. We don't see the wind, but we can feel it and see it moving. That perspective changed everything for me. Choose to have faith in Him, even when you can't see Him.

Proverbs 3:5-6 says, *"Trust in the Lord with all your heart and do not lean on your own understanding. In all your ways acknowledge Him, and He will make your paths straight."* I had a plan for my life, but then something happened that changed everything. It made me realize that while my plans might be great, God's plans are even greater. When I stopped leaning on myself and started leaning on God, my life changed completely. I want you to start trusting in Him and His plans too.

Matthew 8:26 says, *"He said to them, 'Why are you afraid, you men of little faith?' Then He got up and rebuked the winds and the sea, and it became perfectly calm."* Let me remind you: God doesn't call us to be afraid of the storms in life. Instead, He calls us to have faith in Him. He will calm all your storms—you just need to trust Him.

Challenge: My challenge for you today is this: If you hear someone talking about how big their problems are, tell them, "God is greater." Take time to talk with them and remind them that, even though their battles may be great, God is always greater.

Dive in Deeper: Psalm 37:5 Colossians 3:23 Philippians 4:6-7

Notes:

"The Bible is meant to be bread for daily use, not cake for special occasions."
— Unknown

Day 16

Why It's Important to be in Your Bible

First of all, the Bible is literally the Word of God. It's one of the ways God communicates with us. It shows us how faithful He is and how He is there for us no matter what we go through. The Bible is proof that God is real and that He is a loving God.

Hebrews 4:12: *"For the word of God is living and active and sharper than any two-edged sword, and piercing as far as the division of soul and spirit, of both joints and marrow, and able to judge the thoughts and intentions of the heart."* To me, this verse expresses how incredible the Word of God is. Right there at the beginning, it talks about how the Word of God is living and active, which is so cool because it still lives in us today.

2 Timothy 3:16-17: *"All Scripture is inspired by God and profitable for teaching, for reproof, for correction, for training in righteousness; so that the*

man of God may be adequate, equipped for every good work." This is such a cool verse! To me, it talks about how the Bible comes from God and helps us in whatever we may do in our lives.

Colossians 3:16: *"Let the word of Christ richly dwell within you, with all wisdom teaching and admonishing one another with psalms and hymns and spiritual songs, singing with thankfulness in your hearts to God."* The beginning of this verse speaks to me. It says, *"Let the word of Christ dwell richly within you."* To me, this means to let God's Word be fully within you and in everything you do. I try to remember how God speaks to us through these verses when I am speaking to others.

From my personal experience, reading God's Word has helped me become so much closer to Him. God speaks to us in different ways. Sometimes, it's through the Bible; sometimes, it's through prayer; sometimes, it's just out of the blue! And also, from personal experience, when I am not in my Bible very often, I feel so far from God. When I read my Bible, it helps me strengthen my relationship with Him! It also helps me to know who God is. Sometimes, the enemy will feed you lies about who God is, but the Bible shows us who God really is.

Challenge: I challenge you to memorize one Bible verse today. Find one that you really like, and remember it during hard times. God's Word is the best weapon in battle.

Dive in Deeper: John 1:1, John 17:17, Romans 15:4, Romans 10:17

Rose Patton

Notes:

"Patience is not simply the ability to wait – it's how we behave while we're waiting."
— Joyce Meyer

Day 17

Learning to be Patient

I talk a lot about the injury I went through because it was a big change in my life. While I was injured, I had to learn to trust God and be patient. I often found myself asking God, "Why is this happening to me? Why me?" I might not have the full answer yet, but I can see that God changed my life in the way I needed. All I had to do was be patient and trust Him. Every day, He proves to me that His plan is better than mine in every way.

I don't know about you, but I struggle to be patient. I struggle with waiting for things to change or waiting for things to happen. Being patient is hard, but it's important. Sometimes God makes you wait because you might not be ready for what's ahead. In John 16:12, Jesus says, *"I have many more things to say to you, but you cannot bear them now."* He won't put anything on you that you can't handle, so don't get angry at God for not doing what you want in your life. You just might not be ready.

I feel like being patient has a lot to do with trusting. When you patiently wait for God to get you through a storm, you are trusting Him. You shut out every doubt and give your heart fully to Him. We need to learn to give Him every big thing and every little thing. His timing is better than ours in every way, so give Him your plans and trust His timing—because He is in control, not you.

Colossians 3:12 says, *"So, as those who have been chosen of God, holy and beloved, put on a heart of compassion, kindness, humility, gentleness, and patience."* Let's focus on the word "patience." God calls us to have patience. Even though we can't always see how everything will turn out, we can trust God to get us through. Jesus has already won every battle you will ever face by dying on the cross for you. Even if you don't know the outcome, trust that God has already worked everything out. Be patient; just because you can't see things happening doesn't mean they aren't.

Psalm 27:14 says, *"Wait for the Lord; be strong, and let your heart take courage. Yes, wait for the Lord."* To me, this verse is a reminder to wait for the Lord in whatever we are doing. Trust His plan. It might take some time, but "wait for the Lord." I can testify that even when it doesn't make sense, God is working. There will be times when you want to question Him. But I can also testify that everything—and I mean EVERYTHING—He is doing in your life is for a purpose, even if you have to wait to see it.

Challenge: Today, I want you to write down five times God made you wait, but the outcome was greater than you ever could have dreamed. Use this as a reminder to let God take control, because He will make it even better.

Dive in Deeper: Ecclesiastes 7:8, James 1:2-4 (pay close attention to verse 3), and Lamentations 3:25-26

Rose Patton

Notes:

"Spoiler, God wins!!"
— Unknown

Day 18

Learning to Respect Others

It can be difficult to respect others. I struggled with it for a while, but I'm getting better at it. I totally understand that you might not want to be respectful to others—I know how that feels. But we are called to treat others the way we want to be treated. So, if you want respect, show it to others!

Respecting others doesn't always mean allowing them into our lives in a deep or personal way. We can respect people from a distance, especially when setting boundaries is necessary to protect our peace and well-being. We should be friendly and love our neighbor, but that doesn't mean we have to tolerate behavior that isn't healthy for us or pulls away from God.

1 Peter 2:17-18: *"Honor all people, love the brotherhood, fear God, honor the king. Servants, be submissive to your masters with all respect, not only to those who are good and gentle, but also to those who*

are unreasonable." A big part I want to pull out here is the fact that it tells us to respect everyone. Whether they are nice to us or mean, they still deserve our love and respect.

Matthew 7:12: *"In everything, therefore, treat people the same way you want them to treat you, for this is the Law and the Prophets."* This verse literally says to treat people the same way you want them to treat you. If you don't respect others, don't expect them to respect you! We all have people we don't agree with, but even if we don't see eye to eye, we still need to respect them and their views.

That being said, respecting someone doesn't mean you have to keep associating with them if it's pulling you away from God. Boundaries are so important. You can respect someone from a distance without letting them have access to your heart or your life in ways that aren't healthy. Loving others doesn't mean we have to tolerate behavior that doesn't honor God. Sometimes, respecting others means protecting your peace and setting those healthy boundaries.

1 Peter 3:15: *"But in your hearts revere Christ as Lord. Always be prepared to give an answer to everyone who asks you to give the reason for the hope that you have. But do this with gentleness and respect."* This verse pulls out so many different things, but I want to focus on the fact that we are called to be ready to speak out. But in doing so, we need to show gentleness and respect. Treat people the way Jesus treated them. Jesus didn't always have people who liked Him. I mean, He was literally hung on a cross. But no matter what, He still showed them love.

When I started my podcast and began speaking, some people told me they disagreed with what I was saying. And I am okay with that; God gave us all the choice to believe what we choose. Even if we don't agree with someone's decisions or choices, we need to love and respect them. Jesus died on the cross for them, too. Now, every time I look at someone, I think, "Wow, Jesus died for that person, and Jesus loves them so much. So I need to love them and respect them, too." You might be the only part of Jesus that some people see in life, so treat people the way God treats you. Forgive them the way God has forgiven you. Respect them, no matter what.

Challenge: Today, I challenge you to sit down and think about some ways you can start respecting people more, even if it means setting boundaries. Then take that into action, and start respecting others—not just today, but every day.

Dive in Deeper: Romans 12:10, Ephesians 4:2, Philippians 2:3-4, Colossians 3:12-14.

Notes:

"God isn't asking you to figure it out, He is asking you to trust that He already has."
— Unknown

Day 19

Trusting God

It's hard to trust God sometimes, and that's usually because we're human, and someone has come along and made it hard for us to trust. I fully understand that. But the great thing about God is that He is faithful! God loves you, and because of that, He wants what is best for you! If you need a reminder that God loves you, here it is: 1 Thessalonians 1:4—*"We know, dear brothers and sisters, that God loves you and has chosen you to be His own people."*

I also want to remind you that God truly desires what's best for you. But trusting God doesn't mean you'll always get exactly what you want. It means you'll get something even better—what you need.

Proverbs 3:5-6 says, *"Trust in the Lord with all of your heart and do not lean on your own understanding. In all your ways acknowledge Him, and He will make your paths straight."* You might think you know what's best for you, but the truth is, you can't see the whole story. God does. As humans, we can't possibly understand everything God is doing for us. So instead, we get to have faith and trust in Him. He will lead you on the right path, but you have to choose to follow Him.

Romans 15:13 says, *"Now may the God of hope fill you with all joy and peace in believing, so that you will abound in hope by the power of the Holy Spirit."* I've learned that whenever we trust God and choose to believe in Him, He gives us peace and joy. Life is still going to be hard, but God makes it bearable. When we trust Him, we're allowing ourselves to give it all to God and put everything in His hands.

2 Corinthians 5:7 says, *"For we walk by faith, not by sight."* We can't always see what will happen in our lives, but we can choose to have faith that no matter what, God is still good. There are going to be times in your life when you can't see the way out of whatever you're going through. But just because you can't see it doesn't mean it isn't there.

I've had so many moments where I've sat alone asking God, "What are You doing?!?!?! This is not what I thought my life would look like." But the truth is, God gave you this life, so I promise you that you can trust Him with it. I've had moments where I just had to give everything to God. Learning to trust Him wasn't always easy, but it was always worth it. God gives you a choice—He will never force you to trust Him. But please, just try. Your life will start to change for the better!

Challenge: Pray today that you can give everything to God and learn to trust Him. I promise you it will be worth it. He wants to hear from you, so please talk to Him. He is there for you at 6 PM, noon, and even 2 AM. He is there for you 24/7, wherever you are. TRUST HIM!

Dive in Deeper: Psalm 31:14, John 12:44, 1 Corinthians 1:9.

Rose Patton

Notes:

Rose Patton

***"God is good; just add another 'o'."
— Inspired by Tucker Latimer***

Day 20

The Power of Asking for Help

Asking for help is actually such a brave and strong thing to do. There are situations I wouldn't have made it through if I hadn't asked for help. We aren't meant to live life alone, and we will never go through anything alone. Matthew 28:20, "*Teaching them to observe all that I commanded you; and lo, I am with you always, even to the end of the age.*" reminds us that no matter where we go in life, we cannot go anywhere God isn't. He never wants us to feel like we're going through anything alone. Even if you feel like you can't talk to anyone else, talk to God, for His love never fails.

Galatians 6:2 says, *"Bear one another's burdens, and thereby fulfill the law of Christ."* Whenever I am at my worst, I find talking to others really helpful. Many of my friends are strong in their faith, and they've helped me become stronger in mine. So, if you're having trouble or are in a rough place in life, ask for help or guidance, whether from someone in your church or a close friend. But definitely talk to God. Trust me, there are people who care and want to help you.

Ecclesiastes 4:9-10 says, *"Two are better than one because they have a good return for their labor. For if either of them falls, the one will lift up his companion. But woe to the one who falls when there is not another to lift him up."* When you ask for help and allow others to help you, you don't have to carry the load all by yourself. Find people who help lift you up when you fall. And God is there for you, so lean on Him when you don't feel like anyone else understands—He does.

James 1:5 says, *"But if any of you lacks wisdom, let him ask of God, who gives to all generously and without reproach, and it will be given to him."* God will give you what you need. Asking for help is never a bad thing.

Challenge: Today, I challenge you to write down why you feel like you can't ask for help. This will help you overcome the fear of asking for help and allow you to feel more comfortable asking other believers to help bear your burdens. You aren't meant to go through anything alone.

Dive in Deeper: Proverbs 11:14, Psalm 121:1-2, Matthew 7:7

Rose Patton

Notes:

"Everything will be okay in the end. If it's not okay, it's not the end."
— John Lennon

Day 21

Walk Away

Sometimes, we must let God take something out of our lives so He can bless us with something even greater. I want to remind you that everything God does has purpose and meaning. Every time I've gone through a trial or a struggle, I've been able to help someone else. I can testify that yes, your trial may be great, but God's plan is greater.

I reached a point in my life where I was so exhausted because I was in relationships and situations that were just stealing my peace. And let me tell you, if something is hurting you or pulling you away from God, then let God have it. I've learned that my relationship with God is the most important thing in my life.

Trent Shelton once told me, *"Goals are something you reach for, but standards are something you live by."* I give you permission to have standards in your life. I'm not saying to be mean to people who don't meet your standards, but I am saying don't be afraid to let God take them out of your life.

1 Corinthians 15:33 says, *"Do not be deceived: 'Bad company corrupts good morals.'"* This reminds me of something my youth pastor once told me: *"Just because they are good to you doesn't mean they are good for you."* Someone may be nice to you, but then you notice they are drawing you away from Christ. If they don't make you more like Christ, take a step back and see who they are really making you more like—the enemy.

Proverbs 13:20 says, *"He who walks with wise men will be wise, but the companion of fools will suffer harm."* The people you spend your time with will affect who you become. Just like Proverbs 27:17 says, *"Iron sharpens iron, so one man sharpens another."* This reminds us that people will rub off on us. So, ask yourself: Are they making you more like Christ or more like the world?

Matthew 10:14 says, *"Whoever does not receive you nor heed your words, as you go out of that house or that city, shake the dust off your feet."* Don't expect everyone to understand you or believe in your vision. I've learned that, many times, the people you thought were your friends don't believe in your vision. But that's okay because God didn't give them the vision—so don't expect them to see it. If they are taking you away from the vision God has given you, let God take them away.

Philippians 3:13 says, *"Brethren, I do not regard myself as having laid hold of it yet; but one thing I do: forgetting what lies behind and reaching forward to what lies ahead."* This verse is such a good reminder not to look back on relationships, friendships, and situations. Instead, move forward because God has even more in store for you. Your story isn't over yet!

Challenge: Today, I challenge you to write down five things you feel like you need to let go of—whether they are people, situations, or anything else. Then, write down why you feel like you need to let go of them. After that, pray over it.

Dive in Deeper: Proverbs 4:23, Romans 12:18, Colossians 3:2

Rose Patton

Notes:

"I'm a big believer that God CALLS us to do things and then He QUALIFIES us to be able to accomplish those things."
— Russell Brunson

Day 22

Failing Forward

At one point in my life, hearing the words "failure" or "mistake" would have made me cry. I had gotten so wrapped up in what the world had to say about me that I forgot what God had to say about me. I had this idea in my head that if I made one mistake, I *was* a mistake. But God reminds us that that's not the case at all.

Proverbs 24:16 says, *"For a righteous man falls seven times, and rises again, but the wicked stumble in time of calamity."* This reminded me that, yes, we are going to fall—but we are called to get back up. I no longer think that when I fall, I am a failure. Instead, I know that when I fall, I get the chance to rise even stronger.

1 John 1:9 says, *"If we confess our sins, He is faithful and righteous to forgive us our sins and to cleanse us from all unrighteousness."* Whenever we make a mistake or mess up, we can ask for

forgiveness. Christ knew we were going to make mistakes; we aren't perfect.

Hebrews 12:11 says, *"All discipline for the moment seems not to be joyful, but sorrowful; yet to those who have been trained by it, afterwards it yields the peaceful fruit of righteousness."* Mistakes aren't going to feel joyful, but take those mistakes and allow them to grow you closer to God. Use your mistakes as a way to grow in your faith.

Philippians 3:13 says, *"Brethren, I do not regard myself as having laid hold of it yet; but one thing I do: forgetting what lies behind and reaching forward to what lies ahead."* Don't focus on the mistakes you've made, because then you might miss all of the blessings God has given you through those mistakes. Let the mistakes teach you, and let them help you grow.

Challenge: Today, I challenge you to use your mistakes and failures—don't let them use you. Learn from every situation.

Dive in Deeper: Romans 3:23, Psalm 103:12, Romans 5:3-5

Rose Patton

Notes:

"If Jesus can rise from the dead, you can rise from the bed, go to church."
— Unknown

Day 23

Why Prayer is so Powerful

Prayer is something that is so important to me. It is a way for me to talk to God. When I pray, I can feel God there with me, and that is so beautiful. It's a reminder that you are never alone and that He is always there for you, no matter what you do. Prayer is so cool because you can do it no matter where you are or what you're doing—whether you're in the car, at school, or just in bed at night.

When I have been at my worst moments, especially when I was injured, I needed someone to talk to. But sometimes, I felt like I couldn't explain my pain to my friends or family because they didn't understand. But guess who did? God. He heard every fear and every worry; He listened every time I cried out. And He never left my side.

1 Thessalonians 5:17 says, *"Pray without ceasing."* We are going to go through so many things where we feel like we don't want to tell

anyone. But in those situations, that is when we need to cling to God and pray. He hears you, and He loves you. So talk to Him through every up and down. He wants to be there with you in every situation.

I want to remind you that when you pray, you don't need to hide anything from God. The truth is, He already knows. But I find that telling Him the things I'm going through, even if I am ashamed of them, helps me get it out. God is the best therapist! Another thing to remember is that God can see through your fake prayers. He can tell if you're being truthful with Him rather than just saying what you think you should say. Be honest and be open.

Mark 11:24 says, *"Therefore I say to you, all things for which you pray and ask, believe that you have received them, and they will be granted you."* This verse is so cool because Jesus tells us that we will receive what we pray for. But I want to remind you that you might not get what you prayed for that same day. Trust God's timing!

Prayer is a one-on-one conversation with God. Talking to God is so important. You may not always feel like you are being heard, but I can testify that God is listening, and He is there with you ALWAYS.

Challenge: Set aside 10 minutes today to pray. Find a quiet spot, and talk to God about everything on your heart—your worries, your joys, and even the things you're struggling with. Be honest and open. Then, take a moment to just sit in His presence and listen. Trust that He is there, hearing you and loving you.

If you feel led, write down your prayers in a journal and look back on them later to see how God has been working in your life!

Dive in Deeper: James 5:16, Luke 5:16, Romans 12:12.

Notes:

"Jesus died for you in public, don't just live for Him in private."

— Unknown

Day 24

Being Content

Being content with what God has given us in our lives can be hard, especially when you see all these people with "perfect lives" on social media. But never compare your journey to someone else's. We are each at a different point in our stories, and we will never have the same story as anyone else. Your story is unique because it's yours. Let God take the lead and be content, knowing that He is in control and everything happening is happening for a reason.

Philippians 4:11: *"Not that I speak from want, for I have learned to be content in whatever circumstances I am."* Here, Paul is sharing how he has learned to be content, no matter the circumstance. This is how we should be too. But contentment is something we must learn. You will go through trials where you must learn to be content and trust God to provide for you.

Hebrews 13:5: *"Make sure that your character is free from the love of money, being content with what you have; for He Himself has said, 'I will never desert you, nor will I ever forsake you.'"* This is such a great verse. We don't need to worry about how much money we have because we have God. And God promises that He will never leave us. Money comes and goes, but God never leaves. Learn to lean on God, not money or possessions.

Ecclesiastes 5:10: *"He who loves money will not be satisfied with money, nor he who loves abundance with its income. This too is vanity."* We are reminded here that if we chase money, we will never be satisfied. You will spend your life chasing something that will never fulfill you or make you truly happy. Spend your life living for God, not for money. And be content with what you have. If you have a million dollars, awesome—be grateful for that. And if you have two dollars, be grateful for that too. No matter the circumstance, be grateful and content, knowing that God is still good, and He will provide for you.

Challenge: Take a moment today to write down at least five things you're grateful for. Focus on the blessings you already have, rather than what you don't have. By shifting your attention to the good things in your life, you'll begin to grow more content. Ask God to help you see the ways He has already provided for you.

Dive in Deeper: 2 Corinthians 12:9-10, Luke 12:15, Matthew 6:31-33.

Rose Patton

Notes:

"You cannot fix what you are unwilling to face."

— Garret J. White

Day 25

God's Approval vs The World's Approval

I have had so many moments where I just wanted someone else's approval. But the world is full of lies, while God tells the truth. If you go to the world for approval, it will lie to you, but God will always tell you the truth. And God's opinion of you is the only one that matters. The world will hate you, so don't seek approval from something that hates you. Instead, know that you are loved and worthy because God is love.

Galatians 1:10: *"For am I now seeking the favor of men or of God? Or am I striving to please men? If I were still trying to please men, I would not be a bondservant of the Lord."* This verse is so important. We aren't here for people to like us or to be pleased by what we do. We are here to please God. We shouldn't strive to make people like us because God doesn't just like us—He loves us.

Romans 12:2: *"And do not be conformed to this world, but be transformed by the renewing of your mind, so that you may prove what the will of God is, that which is good and acceptable and perfect."* We aren't called here to be like the world; we are called to be like Christ and to show the world how good He is.

Colossians 3:23: *"Whatever you do, do your work heartily, as for the Lord rather than for men."* You are working for God, not others, so why would you look for approval from others instead of from God?

1 Thessalonians 2:4: *"But just as we have been approved by God to be entrusted with the gospel, so we speak, not as pleasing men, but God who examines our hearts."* Don't live to please men; live to please God, because He is the only one who will ever truly know you.

Why would you let someone who doesn't truly know you tell you your worth? The world will lie to you and make you think that you are not "cool" or not "pretty" enough. Then, you'll get caught in a spiral of worrying about whether you are good enough. But if you would just listen to God, you would realize that you are fearfully and wonderfully made, that you were created for a purpose, and that you are not meant to be like anyone else.

Challenge: Today, when you feel the urge to seek approval from others, stop and remind yourself that God's opinion of you is the only one that truly matters. Take a moment to reflect on your worth in His eyes—loved, chosen, and called for a purpose. If you catch yourself comparing to others or wondering if you're "good enough," replace those thoughts with God's truth: you are fearfully and wonderfully made. Walk in that confidence today, knowing that His approval is the only one that lasts.

Dive in Deeper: Matthew 6:1, John 12:43, Proverbs 29:25

Rose Patton

Notes:

"Consider how valuable your soul must be that God and the devil are both after it."
— C.S. Lewis

Day 26

You Are Forgiven

So far in my life, I have sinned a lot. I sin every day. But guess what? God forgives me every day. No matter how great the sin is, God has forgiven you. There is NOTHING you could ever do to separate yourself from the love and forgiveness of Christ. 1 John 1:9 says, "If we confess our sins, He is faithful and righteous to forgive us our sins and to cleanse us from all unrighteousness." This verse is pretty straightforward. I think it's so beautiful that He will always forgive us. We don't deserve that. But God gives us forgiveness every moment of every day. Romans 5:8 says, *"But God demonstrates His own love toward us, in that while we were yet sinners, Christ died for us."* This is such a special verse. I like to think a lot about how we don't deserve God's forgiveness. Jesus died on the cross, knowing that we would still fall short and mess up every day. He died for YOU even though you don't deserve that. Don't take that for granted. Repent and go back to God. Isaiah 1:18 says, *"Come now, let us reason together,"* says the Lord, *"Though your sins are as scarlet, they will be as white as snow; though they are red like crimson, they will be like wool."* When you give your sins up to Christ, repent, and turn back to Him, you will be a new creation. No matter what you have done in the past, God has forgiven you. I know we all have some things that make us think, *"God, You couldn't possibly forgive me. I've done so much wrong."* Well, here's the thing: John 8:36 tells us, *"So if the Son makes you free, you will be free indeed."* So no matter what you have done, Christ has forgiven you. Don't let your past mistakes make you feel like you can't be forgiven. You are free indeed! The old you has died. Yes, you are still a sinner, but that is why Jesus died for you. He knew that nothing you would ever do could make up for the sins you would commit, so He took your punishment in full by dying on the cross. You will never be able to deserve what Jesus did for you. But yet, He knows that, and He still wants a relationship with you. He has already chosen you; now it's your choice whether you choose Him.

Challenge: Today, I challenge you to reflect on God's forgiveness. Think about the mistakes you've carried and remember that Christ has already forgiven you—no sin is too great for His grace. Write down one area where you need to accept His forgiveness, release it to Him, and pray for His help to fully embrace the freedom He offers. Choose to walk in the new life He has given you.

Dive in Deeper: Psalm 103:12, Micah 7:18-19, Ephesians 1:7.

Rose Patton

Notes:

"Make Jesus your first priority, not your last resort."

— *Unknown*

Day 27

Praise the Lord

Sometimes, things happen in our lives, and we feel like we can take the credit and say, "Look at what I did." But that's the wrong way to look at it. I used to struggle with this, but then I realized that I wouldn't be where I am without God. So, instead of saying, "Look what I did," I choose to say, "Look what God has done through me," because I would be nothing without God.

Ephesians 3:20-21 says, *"Now to Him who is able to do far more abundantly beyond all that we ask or think, according to the power that works within us, to Him be the glory in the church and in Christ Jesus to all generations forever and ever. Amen."*

Christ is so awesome. He does amazing things that we can't even comprehend. I can testify that He has changed my life and given me more blessings than I could ever count. I give Him all the glory.

Matthew 5:16 says, *"Let your light shine before men in such a way that they may see your good works, and glorify your Father who is in heaven."* We are told to let His light shine through us. We show others how He has saved our lives and how we give Him all the credit for how far we've come.

Romans 11:36 says, *"For from Him and through Him and to Him are all things. To Him be the glory forever. Amen."*

Everything was created by and for God. God created you, and He deserves your praise. You are so unique and awesome because God made you that way. He created you different from anyone else, and that's a good thing. You are unique, and God deserves your praise for that.

John 15:8 says, *"My Father is glorified by this, that you bear much fruit, and so prove to be My disciples."*

We glorify God when we do what He has called us to do. God gives each of us a calling, and we have a choice: follow Him or walk away because of fear that it won't work out. But think about how you can glorify God when you follow His plan and pursue the vision He has given you.

No matter what you do in life, thank God for His help. You wouldn't be where you are without Him. Don't take Him for granted!

Challenge: Today, I challenge you to write down five things you've accomplished that you're super proud of. Then, write down how each of those things happened because God gave you the opportunity, the vision, and the strength.

Dive in Deeper: 2 Corinthians 3:18, John 7:18, 1 Corinthians 6:19-20

Notes:

"Be the change that you wish to see in the world."
— Mahatma Gandhi

Day 28

Love Like Jesus

I know we've all had times when we didn't want to love someone. But God calls us to love, even when it's hard. I mean, Jesus still loved and forgave the people who hung Him on the cross and crucified Him. So, I know you can love and forgive the people who are talking bad about you or making fun of you. You don't have to let them keep hurting you, but you need to love them.

I had people in my life who weren't super great to me. They said a lot of lies about me, and that made me mad. But I went to the Bible, and it told me to love them anyway. I chose to love them, and they realized that loving others is so much better than being mean.

1 John 4:19 says, *"We love because He first loved us."* God loves us so much—so much that He sent His only Son to die for you (John 3:16). God loves you even though you don't deserve

His love, so you need to love everyone, even if you think they don't deserve it. We all need love. And who knows, you could be the only bit of love someone has in their life.

1 John 4:7-8 says, *"Beloved, let us love one another, for love is from God; and everyone who loves is born of God and knows God. The one who does not love does not know God, for God is love."* Whenever I talk to God or sing songs of worship, I feel so happy and loved. When you know God, you will know love. And you will be able to share God's love more. God is love, and He has called us here to love others.

Galatians 5:13-14 says, *"For you were called to freedom, brethren; only do not turn your freedom into an opportunity for the flesh, but through love serve one another. For the whole law is fulfilled in one word, in the statement, 'You shall love your neighbor as yourself.'"* That last statement says to "love your neighbor as yourself." Now, that can be hard. I've found that trying to remember that you and they are equal helps. God loves you both the same. So, you need to love everyone the way you love yourself.

Challenge: If someone offends you today, practice showing grace. Instead of holding on to hurt, choose to respond with love and understanding. Remember, God shows us grace every day.

Dive in Deeper: 1 John 4:11, Romans 12:10, Romans 13:8.

Rose Patton

Notes:

"God doesn't give the hardest battles to His toughest soldiers, He creates the toughest soldiers out of life's hardest battles."

— *Unknown*

Day 29

God Will Give You Strength

There are going to be times in your life that are really hard, but God will give you strength through those times. There are things in life that you won't be able to make it through unless you ask God for strength. You aren't meant to do this on your own. Ask God for strength in those hard times—He will help you through it. I'm not saying it will be easy, but you will be at peace, and it will be bearable.

Philippians 4:13: *"I can do all things through Him who strengthens me."*

You will make it through whatever you are going through because He will give you the strength. No matter how hard it may seem, you can make it through—but you have to allow Him to give you strength. You don't have to fight this battle on your own. Give it to God because He is stronger.

Psalm 28:7: *"The Lord is my strength and my shield; my heart trusts in Him, and I am helped; therefore, my heart exults, and with my song, I shall thank Him."*
God literally is your strength. Please don't try to fight this battle on your own. Trust Jesus with this battle. He already won it when He died for you on that cross. Trust that He will get you through this. Let Him be your strength.

Isaiah 40:29: *"He gives strength to the weary, and to him who lacks might He increases power."*
This verse proves that He gives strength to those who are weary. We will all have times when we feel weary, and our burdens will seem too heavy to bear. But trust in Him, and give those worries and burdens to Him. He will take care of them because He is stronger.

1 John 4:4: *"You are from God, little children, and have overcome them; because greater is He who is in you than he who is in the world."*
This verse changed my perspective on my problems. No matter what the world may throw at me, God is still greater. He will give

you the strength you need to overcome this battle. Your battle may be great, but God will always be greater.

I can testify that He will give you the strength you need to make it through whatever you may face. He has done it for me, so I know He can do it for you.

Challenge: For today's challenge, I want you to think about these verses every time you start to feel weak. God will give you the strength you need to get through every battle.

Dive in Deeper: Ephesians 6:10, Psalm 46:1, 2 Corinthians 12:9-10.

Rose Patton

Notes:

"You are going to look back at the end of this year and say God knew exactly what He was doing; His plans are greater than mine."
— Unknown

Day 30

There Is Always Hope

Do you ever feel like, "God, I am so lost and far from You. There is no way You will save me now"? But Romans 10:13 reminds us, *"Everyone who calls on the name of the Lord will be saved."* It doesn't say, "If you have never sinned or fallen short, the Lord will save you." It says, *"Everyone who calls on the name of the Lord will be saved."* God will save you from anything, wherever and whenever—you just have to call upon His name. Not all hope is gone. God is your only hope.

Isaiah 59:1 says, *"Behold, the Lord's hand is not so short that it cannot save, nor His ear so dull that it cannot hear."* No matter where you go, God can save you and pull you out of whatever situation you are in. I promise you—you are not too far away for God to save you. He has rescued me, and I know He can do the same for you.

God is our only hope. When Jesus died on the cross for us, He gave us hope and a second chance. But it's up to us whether we choose to take it.

Psalm 23:4 reminds us, *"Even though I walk through the valley of the shadow of death, I will fear no evil, for You are with me; Your rod and Your staff, they comfort me."* He never leaves you. Even in your hardest moments, when everyone else walks away, He will be with you. He will hold on to you and never let go. I know that sometimes life feels so dark, and you think there is no possible way to make it through. I promise you—it will get better if you give your burdens and your troubles to God.

John 16:33 says, *"These things I have spoken to you, so that in Me you may have peace. In the world you have tribulation, but take courage; I have overcome the world."* No matter how rough the world gets or how bad your situation might seem, God has already overcome it. We have hope, knowing that everything happening now was already known to God—and He has defeated it.

Before you even started fighting this battle, Jesus won it on the cross. Everything you have done and everything you will do was nailed to that cross.

Challenge: Today, I challenge you to give God everything that is holding you back. Hand over the things that are breaking you. He will save you from them, but you have to let Him.

Dive In Deeper: Romans 10:13, Isaiah 43:2, Hebrews 6:19

Rose Patton

Notes:

Look How Far You've Come!

Wow, you made it! Before you close this devotional, take a moment to look back at where you started. Go back to those first notes you wrote down and reflect on all that's happened in these 30 days. How has your walk with Christ grown? What prayers have been answered? What truths have taken root in your heart?

Use this space to write about what God has done in your life during this time. Celebrate the progress you've made, the lessons you've learned, and the ways He's moved in your journey. Let this be a reminder of His faithfulness and a step forward in continuing to grow in your relationship with Him.

You've come so far, and the best is yet to come! Keep walking with Him—you've got this!

Notes:

_____

_____

_____

Rose Patton

Rose Patton

Notes:

Rose Patton

Notes:

Rose Patton

Notes:

Notes:

Notes:

About the Author

Rose Patton is a 14-year-old Christian author, speaker, and host of the *Blessed Bonds* podcast. She is passionate about helping others grow in their faith and follow the unique calling God has placed on their lives. Inspired by her own experiences and her growing relationship with God, Rose realized that God had given her a voice to share His Word and encourage others during their trials.

Through her podcast, she brings on guests to share their stories and life lessons, motivating listeners to live boldly for God. Her favorite scriptures, including Jeremiah 29:11 and Genesis 50:20, remind her of God's promises and the purpose He has for every individual.

Everything Rose does is for the glory of God, and she strives to live by the fruits of the Spirit.

Her ultimate mission is to inspire others to trust God's plan, embrace their faith, and confidently live out the calling He has given them.

Rose Patton

Made in the USA
Middletown, DE
11 February 2025

71150701R00101